# LESS

## —THAN—

# ENTIRELY SANCTIFIED

DOUG HALL

INTERVARSITY PRESS
DOWNERS GROVE, ILLINOIS 60515

InterVarsity Press is the book-publishing division of InterVarsity Christian Fellowship, a student movement active on campus at hundreds of universities, colleges and schools of nursing in the United States of America, and a member movement of the International Fellowship of Evangelical Students. For information about local and regional activities, write Public Relations Dept., InterVarsity Christian Fellowship, 6400 Schroeder Rd., P.O. Box 7895, Madison, WI 53707-7895.

Cover illustration: Doug Hall

ISBN 0-8308-1833-2

Printed in the United States of America ∞

**Library of Congress Cataloging-in-Publication Data**
Hall, Doug, 1956-
    Less than entirely sanctified/by Doug Hall.
        p.    cm.
    ISBN 0-8308-1833-2
    1. Christian life—Caricatures and cartoons.    2. American wit and
humor, Pictorial.    I. Title.
    NC1429.H323A4    1992
    741.5'973—dc20
                                            91-44964
                                                CIP

15    14    13    12    11    10    9    8    7    6    5    4    3    2
03    02    01    00    99    98    97    96    95    94

For Cindy

# Introduction

No great hymns are written about the debates of the church-parking-lot resurfacing committee. Not many sermons lift up the examples of martyred seventh-grade Sunday-school teachers. And little Scripture is expressly devoted to how to feed a hungry family from the church pantry when all that's left is clam dip.

It's our human limitations that create these peculiar opportunities to see God's grace at work. We are fallible human beings trying to respond to a divine call, and that inevitably results in humorous—as well as inspiring—moments. This book is about those moments.*

*Additional note to the reader: If you find anything that's truly funny in this book, I give all the glory to God. If you find anything that's not funny, I blame my editors.

By the time he realized the danger, Carl had developed a compulsive chain-reference habit.

"Welcome to Lake Road Church, 'Where we love everybody' . . . in that macho, moose-killing way we men have, of course!"

"Don't forget! Next Sunday we meet at the church across the street for our annual sheep-stealing competition."

"When you don't believe in written creeds, you have to squeeze a lot of doctrine into your name."

"I want to make a public confession to my brothers and sisters
in the church. The rest of the world will have to buy my book for $14.95."

"Actually, nobody considers that to be a significant theological issue anymore . . . although it was the reason our denomination was first formed."

"The rest of the staff feels you underestimate the ministry potential of your license plates."

"Maybe we need to go liturgical for a few Sundays."

"Our banners today were made by Matthew Ebbert, who really needs to talk with a caring adult."

"Tonight's service is at 7:00 Eastern Time. That's 6:00 Central Time for you folks back in the balcony."

"He tried to steal my joy."

"Harriet! What time is that show that's corrupting our young people?!"

"Lord, guide our hearts and hands as we strive to make a *real killing* in the market."

"When we serve, we serve. When we fundraise, we fundraise."

Three minutes into the Seminary Bowl, "Yahweh's Finest" gets a 15-yard penalty for heresy.

Mrs. Frottering didn't realize that organizing the primary department Easter egg hunt would lead to charges of blatant secularism.

Equipped with the best manuals, workbooks and tapes, the Wilsons go off to work on their marriage.

Later analysis concluded that "Worship on Ice" failed because it required gifts not listed in 1 Corinthians 12.

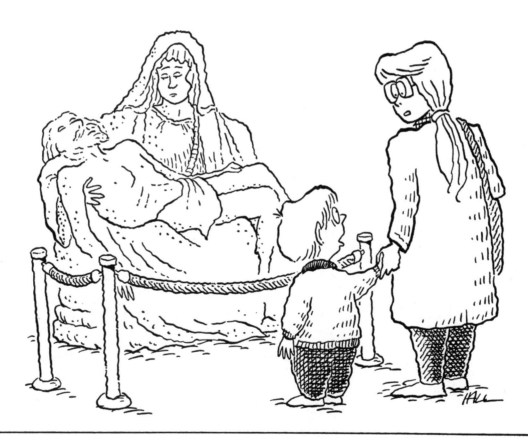

"That's supposed to be Madonna?"

"We probably *did* give simplistic answers to your questions. You were five years old!"

The Children's Crusade of 1212 A.D. faltered when 98% of the volunteers showed up without signed permission slips.

The inevitable questions opened the door to Vern's "Warmed by the Love of God" testimony.

By the time the youth budget accounting error was discovered, attendance had risen 300%.

Mert Thompson was listening to Christian music and reading Christian cartoons
in a Christian magazine while surrounded by Christian wall-coverings.

"Your furnace is pretty outdated. I can see the footprints of Shadrach, Meshach and Abednego."

At some point, Seepage Mill Church decided to "quit playing the numbers game."
OH... YOU'RE NEWCOMERS. OUR "STRANGERS AND ALIENS" CLASS MEETS DOWNSTAIRS IN THE BOILER ROOM.
HOST
HALL

"We are looking for the source of all evil, and we've narrowed it down to this address."

"Fourth graders *love* visual aids."

"Since all the kids wanted a leading role, tonight's Christmas pageant will feature nine Josephs and eight Marys."

"The committee listed all the qualities needed in an effective youth pastor. . . .
I wouldn't let a person like this into my house."

"Since we don't have any women on the faculty at the moment, you female students
will be pleased to hear that Mrs. Muscovitz has agreed to be your mentor."

"As you see on your handouts, today's topic is original sin."

"Well, I see *everybody* has ideas about what they'd like to see in our new building."

"They asked me to say something about Sunday school, but I'm going to talk about my pet lizard, Groucho, instead."

"Willard, I'm starting to question your interpretation of those passages about submission."

"Jimmy, we're the Pastor-Parish Relations Committee, and we'd like to ask you a few questions about your dad."

"I'm sorry for what I've done . . . even though some people think my little imperfections make me more endearing."

"Are you questioning my authority again, Mrs. Thundermuffin?"

"A man from 'Ripley's Believe It or Not!' wants a picture of someone on fire for the Lord."

"This is my fourth sermon on the transforming power of the gospel. Why do you look like the same old bunch?"

"Let me get this straight. After we're married and you graduate from seminary, I'll need to move **anywhere you're** called, chair the missionary society, and help kids make puppets out of milk cartons and **velcro?**"

"Esther has the gift of hospitality."

"Couldn't I talk to a burning bush or something?"

"People were slow in leaving the building until I switched from yelling
'Fire!' to 'Who wants to teach Sunday school?' "

5:27 P.M. — S.W. SNEEDLAP REMEMBERS HE WAS CREATED JUST A LITTLE LOWER THAN THE ANGELS.

"We hate to keep bothering you, Bob, but there's a struggling congregation in Akron that needs an interim."

"That's the situation, Rev. Barlowe. I was going to phone the police,
but then I thought, 'No, what they need is a pastoral call.'"

"Liturgical dance was the worship committee's idea."

"God may have already accepted you, but *our* standards are just a little **higher**."

After a very brief discussion, the board of trustees dismissed Herb's charge
that the church had become infatuated with youth.

Church council meetings always ran more smoothly when opened with a season of both **prayer** and **bumper cars.**

"I don't want to tell you who to witness to, but the choir needs a mezzo-soprano."

"I encourage the whole congregation to attend tonight's city-wide unity service.
It'll give us a chance to scope out the competition."

Fruit flies pass through the teen years in four intense hours.

"We've been meeting for fifty years, but we never quite found a good time to change our name."

Pastor Weintraube decides the new lighting system needs a dimmer switch.

CHURCH
OF THE
TRIPLE
SPIRE

HALL

"We don't have a *formal* church-planting program, but somehow we manage a nasty split *every few years*."

"Maybe we should have hired an architect who'd designed something other than strip malls."

"1994 is the year we bring the entire planet to Christ. 1995 is the year we party."

"Sorry, I don't encourage discussion in this seminar. I find that questions disrupt the flow of my answers."

Late at night in the gloom of his castle tower, the evil
Dr. Mordrek composes new unsingable tunes for old favorite hymns.

"I *know* he said to let the little kids come to him, but I really think he'd want Andrew or somebody to handle the junior highs."

"Lord, I lay before you the prayer concerns voiced this morning . . .
even though most of 'em sound like *whining* to me."

"Denominational headquarters has officially added Stewardship Sunday to the ecclesiastical calendar."

"Our church-building work camp demonstrated an unprecedented commitment to missions in that area."

"Can we talk? The topic is either music or my life-destroying rejection by Becky Hathaway . . . *your choice.*"

"God wants to speak to you. Consult your local listings."

"Brad just scored another plumbing victory. We'll be up celebrating 'til dawn."

Atomic alto Gladys Thundermuffin takes an unauthorized whack
at a solo interpretation of the "Hallelujah Chorus."

"He's always nice, but I know what he's thinking—'this kid only gave $1.23 last year.' "

December 24: The Gleanors find themselves possessed by the Christmas spirit.

"For some reason, our kids think church is a drag and don't want to come. We need you to lure 'em in and trap 'em."

Minutes later, *everyone* wanted to experience the feeling of wind between their toes.

"Great news, little brother! I just sold you to raise 'Bucks for Bangladesh.' "

"Ms. Simmons? The program people are at my east door, and the building people are at my west door. I'm going to lunch."

"We don't want him to watch programs featuring violence, sex or any of the preachers on this list."

"I want to thank our friends in the sewing circle for their lovely gift to the youth."

"The chairman of the trustees flipped out, flew to Las Vegas and gambled away the church. Our new pastor, Eddie 'The Knife' LaRue, is waiting outside."

"I don't remember *all* ten commandments, but I know I'm not supposed to take off my **shoes during the service** unless I just changed my socks."

"To be honest, Preacher, we were expecting a little more reassurance that Nick's soul is out there partying somewhere."

"They're always eager to get into the woods during deer season. Just don't say anything controversial."

"No, Mrs. Thundermuffin. The reason we believe salvation is based on grace instead of works isn't because it leaves more time for hobbies."

"Say . . . you're one of the homeless! I saw your cover story in *Newsweek*."

" 'Behold the fowls of the air. . . . Are ye not much better than they?' Who is *ye*?!!"

" 'God is love' . . . a verse apparently out of fashion the year they designed our **sanctuary**."

"Last February in Buffalo, I developed a special burden for Polynesians."

"Do you think we've become ingrown?"

Occasionally, Pastor Wescott's interpretation of Scripture conflicts with the footnotes in Mel's study Bible.

"This sermon is mainly aimed at Ed, but the rest of you might get something out of listening."

"God calls us to evangelism! The bank that holds our mortgage has mentioned it too."